The Goose

A very detailed Amigurum

The Goose Charles

Attention!

This master-class does not contain knitting lessons for beginners. This pattern is designed for those who can already knit and have basic knowledge and experience in crocheting.

Difficulty level – medium.

The size of the finished toy is approx. 9.5 inch*

***The size of the finished toy may vary depending on materials and crochets used.**

Table of Contents

SYMBOLS — 5

LIST OF MATERIALS USED — 6

KNITTING PATTERN — 7

BEAK — 7
HEAD — 8
BODY — 9
TAIL — 11
WINGS — 13
LEGS — 15

CLOTHES — 17

HAT — 17
T-SHIRT — 19
SCARF — 24

ACCESSORIES — 25

BAG — 25
BAGUETTE — 28
CROISSANT — 29

THE GOOSE CHARLES IS READY!!! — 31

Copyright © 2021 by Helena Denisoff

All rights reserved; no part of this publication may be reproduced or transmitted by any means, electronic, mechanical, photocopying, or otherwise, without the prior permission of the publisher.

Symbols

AR – amigurumi ring

CH – chain stitch

Sl St - slipped stitch

Sc – single crochet

Hdc - half double crochet

Wid – knitting widening

Nar – knitting narrowing

(…)*n –the actions in the parentheses should be repeated n times

(N)- a figure in parentheses at the end of the rnd indicates the total number of loops in the rnd

List of Materials Used

Main colors (for the body):

- Yarn 100% acryl 2 oz/220 yd. Color – White. Color – Orange.

Colors for the T-shirt:

- Yarn 100% acryl 2oz/ 220 yd. Color – White. Color – Dark blue.

Color for the hat and scarf:

- Yarn 100% acryl 2oz/220 yd. Color – Dark red.

Color for the bag:

- Yarn 40% acryl 60% cotton 2oz/ 180 yd. Color – Light beige.

Color for the pastry:

- Yarn 55% cotton 45% acryl 2oz/ 175 yd. Color – Mustard.

- Crochet # 2 US Size

- Holofiber / synthetic fluff

- A long sewing needle

- Scissors

- Pins

- Eyes with secure pinning 0.3 inch - 2 buttons with a diameter up to 0.4 inch

Knitting pattern

Beak

Beak is knitted from the main orange color.

Make a chain of 18ch. Make a circle from the chain knitting a sl st into the first loop of the chain.

Rnd 1-2: Start knitting into the same loop that you made sl st from. 18 sc

Rnd 3: (nar,7)*2 (16)

Rnd 4: (nar,6)*2 (14)

Rnd 5: (nar,5)*2 (12)

Rnd 6: 12 sc

Rnd 7: (nar,4)*2 (10)

Rnd 8: (nar,3)*2 (8)

Fasten the thread, cut, leave the ends for sewing.

Fold the beak as shown on the 2nd photo. Using the ends that you left and a needle, sew the fold on the beak, to fix it in this shape.

Head

Knit from the main white yarn.

Rnd 1: 6 sc in AR

Rnd 2: wid*6 (12)

Rnd 3: (1 sc, wid)*6 (18)

Rnd 4: (2 sc, wid)*6 (24)

Rnd 5: (3 sc, wid)*6 (30)

Rnd 6: (4 sc, wid)*6 (36)

Rnd 7: (5 sc, wid)*6 (42)

Rnd 8-35: 42 sc

Knit 6 sc more (new beginning of the rnd)

Don't stuff the detail yet. Sew the beak on and put the eyes in.

The beak should be between the 14-19 rnd (the upper part of the beak in the 14th rnd, and the lower part in the 19th rnd.) Put in the eyes so that they are paralleled with the right and left corner of the beak, at the level of the beak fold, indenting 1 crochet from it. (look at the photo)

Now you can stuff the detail with the filler.

Body

Stuff the body as you knit.

Rnd 1: (6 sc, wid)*6 (48)

Rnd 2: (7 sc, wid)*6 (54)

Rnd 3: (5 sc, wid)*9 (63)

Rnd 4: (6 sc, wid)*9 (72)

Rnd 5: (7 sc, wid)*9 (81)

Rnd 6: (8 sc, wid)*9 (90)

Rnd 7: (8 sc, wid)*10 (100)

Rnd 8-17: 100 sc

Rnd 18: (8 sc, nar)*10 (90)

Rnd 19-20: 90 sc

Rnd 21: (8 sc, nar)*9 (81)

Rnd 22-23: 81 sc

Rnd 24: (7 sc, nar)*9 (72)

Rnd 25-26: 72 sc

Rnd 27: (6 sc, nar)*9 (63)

Rnd 28: 63 sc

Rnd 29: (5 sc, nar)*9 (54)

Rnd 30: 54 sc

Rnd 31: (7 sc, nar)*6 (48)

Rnd 32: (6 sc, nar)*6 (42)

Rnd 33: (5 sc, nar)*6 (36)

Rnd 34: (4 sc, nar)*6 (30)

Rnd 35: (3 sc, nar)*6 (24)

Rnd 36: (2 sc, nar)*6 (18)

Rnd 37: (1 sc, nar)*6 (12)

Rnd 38: nar*6 (6)

Then tighten the hole using a needle. To do this, hook up the front wall of the loop closest to the needle and the front wall of the next loop, pull the thread. Do this till the hole is completely tightened. Fasten the thread, cut, hide the end.

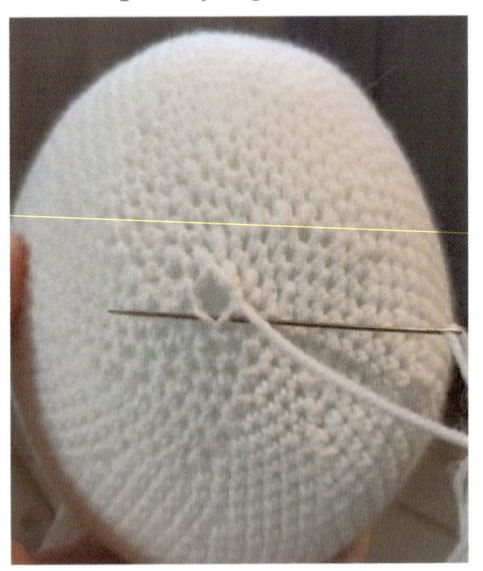

Tail

Rnd 1: 6 sc in AR

Rnd 2: wid*6 (12)

Rnd 3-4: 12 sc

Rnd 5: (1 sc, wid)*6 (18)

Rnd 6: 18 sc

Rnd 7: (2 sc, wid)*6 (24)

Rnd 8: 24 sc

Rnd 9: (3 sc, wid)*6 (30)

Rnd 10: 30 sc

Rnd 11: (4 sc, wid)*6 (36)

Rnd 12: 36 sc

Rnd 13: (5 sc, wid)*6 (42)

Rnd 14: 42 sc

Rnd 15: (6 sc, wid)*6 (48)

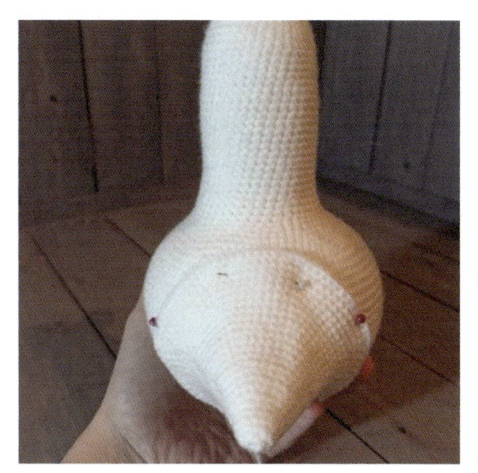

Rnd 16: 48 sc

Rnd 17: (7 sc, wid)*6 (54)

Rnd 18: 54 sc

Rnd 19: (8 sc, wid)*6 (60)

Rnd 20: 60 sc

Rnd 21: (9 sc, wid)*6 (66)

Rnd 22: (10 sc, wid)*6 (72)

Rnd 23: 72 sc

Rnd 24: (11 sc, wid)*6 (78)

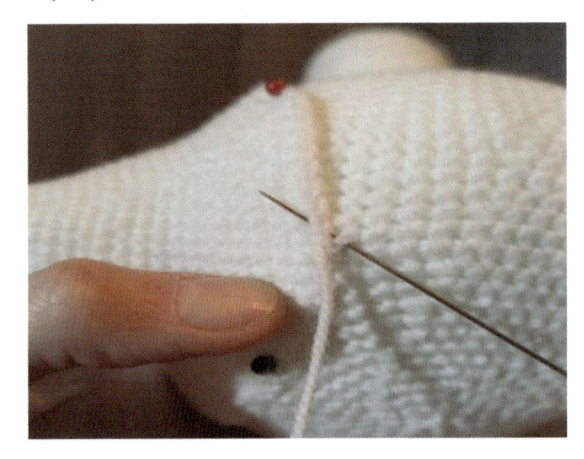

Fasten the thread, cut, leave the ends for sewing.

Sew the tail to the body, place it on the center of the back.

The lower part of the tail should form a straight line with the body (look at the photo).

Stuff the detail as you knit, but leave the end of the tail empty.

Wings

Knit 2 wings.

Rnd 1: 6 sc in AR

Rnd 2: wid*6 (12)

Rnd 3-4: 12 sc

Rnd 5: (1 sc, wid)*6 (18)

Rnd 6-7: 18 sc

Rnd 8: (2 sc, wid)*6 (24)

Rnd 9-10: 24 sc

Rnd 11: (3 sc, wid)*6 (30)

Rnd 12-14: 30 sc

Rnd 15: (4 sc, wid)*6 (36)

Rnd 16-21: 36 sc

Rnd 22: (4 sc, nar)*6 (30)

Rnd 23: (4 sc, nar)*5 (25)

Rnd 24: (3 sc, nar)*5 (20)

Rnd 25: (2 sc, nar)*5 (15)

Rnd 26: (1 sc, nar)*5 (10)

Rnd 27: nar*5 (5)

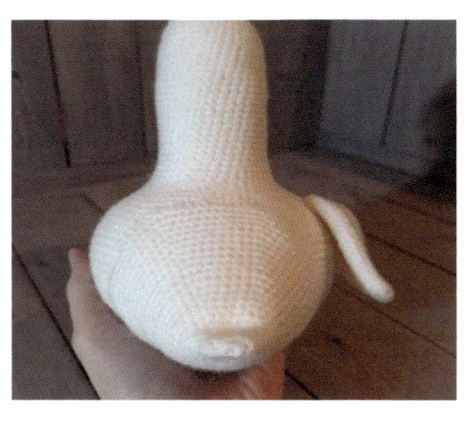

Then tighten the hole using a needle.

Cut the thread leaving the end for sewing.

Sew the wings to the sides of the body positioning them diagonally (the "shoulder" should be higher than the wing tip).

Sew on **only** the shoulder part, 6 rnds lower from the neck.

Legs

Knit 2 legs.

Start knitting from the orange yarn.

Make a chain of 12ch. Start knitting into the 2nd loop from the crochet.

Rnd 1: On one side of the chain-11 sc, on the other- 11 sc. (22)

Rnd 2-4: 22 sc

Rnd 5: (nar, 9 sc)*2 (20)

Rnd 6-7: 20 sc

Rnd 8: (nar, 8 sc)*2 (18)

Rnd 9: (nar, 7 sc)*2 (16)

Rnd 10: (nar, 6 sc)*2 (14)

Then knit the heel. Use swing rnds.

Make 1ch, swing the knitting.

Rnd 1: 7 sc

Rnd 2: nar, 3 sc, nar (5)

Rnd 3: nar, 1 sc, nar (3)

Rnd 4: nar, 1 sc, then 3sc on the lateral side of the leg, 7sc on the front side of the leg, 3 sc on the other lateral side (15)

Then again knit the leg in spiral order.

Rnd 11-19: 15 sc

Change yarn color to white at the end of the 19th rnd.

Rnd 20: wid*15 (30)

Rnd 21-25: 30 sc.

Fasten the thread, cut, leave the ends for sewing.

Thoroughly stuff the legs, leave the feet empty. Knit precisely under the neck with a distance of approx. three loops.

Clothes

Hat

Use red yarn.

Make a chain of 45 ch.

Make a circle from the chain knitting a sl st into the first loop of the chain.

Start knitting from the same loop that you've knitted a sl st into.

Rnd 1: 1 ch, 45 hdc

Rnd 2: through the back wall of the loop (8 sc, wid)*5 (50)

Rnd 3: (9 sc, wid)*5 (55)

Rnd 4: (10 sc, wid)*5 (60)

Rnd 5: (11 sc, wid)*5 (65)

Rnd 6-7: 65 sc

Rnd 8: (11 sc, nar)*5 (60)

Rnd 9: (10 sc, nar)*5 (55)

Rnd 10: (9 sc, nar)*5 (50)

Rnd 11: (8 sc, nar)*5 (45)

Rnd 12: (7 sc, nar)*5 (40)

Rnd 13: (6 sc, nar)*5 (35)

Rnd 14: (5 sc, nar)*5 (30)

Rnd 15: (4 sc, nar)*5 (25)

Rnd 16: (3 sc, nar)*5 (20)

Rnd 17: (2 sc, nar)*5 (15)

Rnd 18: (1 sc, nar)*5 (10)

Rnd 19: nar*5 (5)

Then tighten the hole using a needle.

Make a loop by pulling a thread, fasten the thread, cut, hide the end.

T-shirt

Knit with dark blue and white yarn.

Knit 5 separate details, then sew them together.

Knit all the details using swing rnds, at the end of each rnd knit 1 ch and swing.

Start knitting every detail with dark blue yarn, then change the yarn color each rnd. Crochet round each detail before fastening the thread.

Detail 1-front:

Make 20 ch, knit into the 2nd loop from the crochet.

Rnd 1: 9 hdc, wid, 9 hdc (20)

Rnd 2: wid, 18 hdc, wid (22)

Rnd 3: wid, 20 hdc, wid (24)

Rnd 4: wid, 22 hdc, wid (26)

Rnd 5: wid, 24 hdc, wid (28

Rnd 6: wid, 26 hdc, wid (30)

Rnd 7: wid, 28 hdc, wid (32)

Rnd 8: 16 hdc, wid, 15 hdc (33)

Rnd 9-13: 33 hdc

Fasten the thread, cut and hide the end.

Detail 2-back:

Knit 2 such details.

Make 12 ch, knit into the 2nd loop from the crochet.

Rnd 1: wid*2,10 hdc (14)

Rnd 2: 11 hdc, wid*3 (17)

Rnd 3: wid, 15 hdc, wid (19)

Rnd 4: 18 hdc, wid (20)

Rnd 5: wid*3, 17 hdc (23)

Rnd 6: wid, 20 hdc, wid*2 (26)

Rnd 7: wid*3, 23 hdc (29)

Rnd 8: 27 hdc, wid *2 (31)

Rnd 9: wid*3, 27 hdc, wid (35)

Fasten the thread, cut, leave the ends for sewing.

Detail 3-sleeves:

Knit 2 such details.

Make 7 ch, knit into the 2nd loop from the crochet.

Rnd 1: wid, 4 hdc, wid (8)

Rnd 2: wid, 6 hdc, wid (10)

Rnd 3: wid, 8 hdc, wid (12)

Rnd 4: wid, 10 hdc, wid (14)

Rnd 5: wid, 12 hdc, wid (16)

Rnd 6: wid, 14 hdc, wid (18)

Rnd 7: wid, 16 hdc, wid (20)

Rnd 8: wid, 18 hdc, wid (22)

Rnd 9: wid, 20 hdc, wid (24)

Fasten the thread, cut, leave the ends for sewing.

First, sew the sleeves and the front detail together as shown on the photo below. Ensure that the rnds align.

Then sew on the details of the back. Sew the corner at the lowest sewing point of the sleeve and the front part. Look at the photo.

Then try the details on the toy.

Using pins, mark the place on the back detail where the other part of the sleeve will be sewed on.

Sew it on.

Knit the back detail with buttonholes.

Knit from dark blue yarn.

Knit using sewing rnds, at the end of each rnd knit 1 ch and swing.

Make a chain of 8ch.

Start knitting into the 2nd loop from the crochet.

Rnd 1-2: 7 sc

Rnd 3: 2 sc, 3ch, skip 3 loops, 2 sc

Rnd 4-8: 7 sc

Rnd 9: 2 sc, 3ch, skip 3 loops, 2 sc

Rnd 10-14: 7 sc

Fasten the thread, cut, leave the ends for sewing.

Sew the detail on the left part of the back.

Mark places for buttons using pins.

Sew the buttons on the other half of the back.

Scarf

Knit from red yarn.

Knit using swing rnds.

Make a chain of 100ch.

Rnd 1-2: 100 hdc.

Fasten the thread, cut, hide the end.

Accessories

Bag

Knit from light beige yarn.

Make a chain of 10ch, start knitting into the 2nd loop from the crochet. Knit using sewing rnds.

Rnd 1-3: 9 sc

Then make a chain of 6ch.

Rnd 4: knit sc into the 1 loop of the previous rnd, thus making a ring. Continue knitting rings till the end of the rnd, there should be 9 of them.

Rnd 5: make 6ch, turn the cloth and knit cc to the center (3ch) of the first ring of the previous rnd. Continue knitting like this till the end of the rnd.

Rnd6-23: knit the same as the rnd 5. (9 rings in each rnd)

Rnd 24: collect the cloth for the second placket. Make 1ch, turn the cloth and knit sc to the center of each ring (3ch) of the previous rnd. Continue knitting like this till the end of the rnd. (9 sc)

Rnd 25-26: 9 sc

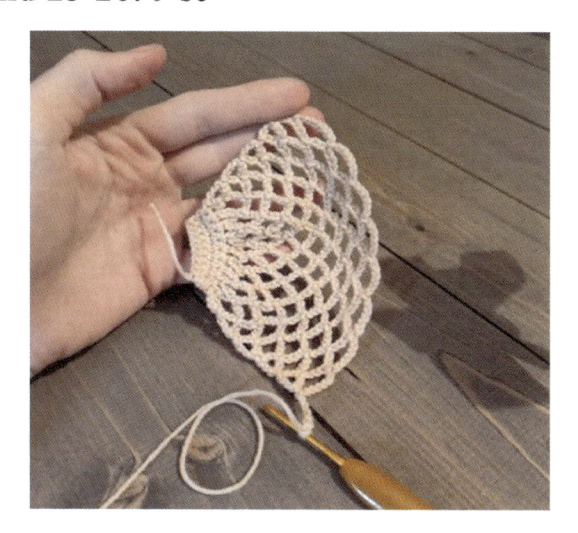

Start knitting in the handles. Make a chain of 44ch. Hook the sl st chain to another corner of the same placket. Then knit 3 sc along the side of the placket.

Then knit a sc in the center of each ring and in the loop between rings all around the bag – a total of 18 sc. We have come to the next placket of the bag. Then knit 3sc on the side part of the second placket.

Again, make 44 ch for the second handle. Connect the chain with another corner of the same placket and knit 3 sc on the side part of the placket.

Knit 18 SC on the other side of the bag, make a circle, and go back to the initial point of knitting – the first handle.

Then mark the beginning of the rnd by the marker ring, and continue knitting on the outer side of the bag 44 sc on the first handle, 3 sc on the lateral side of the placket, 18 sc on the side part of the bag, 3 sc on the other side of the placket, 44 sc on the second handle, 3 sc on the placket, 18 sc on the side part of the bag, 3 sc on the plank and come back to the marker ring.

Fasten the thread, cut and hide the end.

Baguette

Stuff the detail a little bit as you knit.

Knit with the mustard colored yarn.

Rnd 1: 6 sc in AR

Rnd 2: wid*6 (12)

Rnd 3-26: 12 sc

Rnd 27: nar*6 (6)

Fasten the thread, cut, leave the end to sew the hole afterwards. You can also make little "cuts" on your baguette using brown yarn. I also modify the color of the baguette so that it looks more real using dry watercolor.

Croissant

It is also knitted from the mustard colored yarn. Knit 2 such croissants.

Make a chain of 14ch. Start knitting into the 2nd loop from the crochet. Knit using sewing rnds. Knit 1ch at the end of each rnd and swing the work.

Rnd 1: 13 sc

Rnd 2: nar, 9 sc, nar (11)

Rnd 3-4: 11 sc

Rnd 5: nar, 7 sc, nar (9)

Rnd 6: nar, 5 sc, nar (7)

Rnd 7-8: 7 sc

Rnd 9: nar, 3 sc, nar (5)

Rnd 10-12: 5 sc

Rnd 13: nar, 1 sc, nar (3)

Rnd 14-15: 3 sc

Rnd 16: nar, 1 sc (2)

Rnd 17: 2 sc

Rnd 18: nar (1)

Knit the detail around the edge.

Fasten the thread, cut, leave the ends for sewing.

Roll the detail into a tube starting from the long edge to the tip of the triangle. Sew in the end to fix this shape. Form a croissant. You can also sew in the corners of the croissant so that they look folded.

The Goose Charles is ready!!!

Printed in Great Britain
by Amazon